Goddess who takes the form of nine girls from the stars, with the title of queen empresses, these philosophical icons of self-coexistence, in the metaverse of the small blue world are 9 half-steps constituting 3 tritones between two musical notes of a tetrachord in the melodic pattern.

Contents

Preface	*vii*
Prologue	*ix*
1. Verse	1
2. Verse	2
3. Verse	3
4. Verse	4
5. Verse	5
6. Verse	6
7. Verse	7
8. Verse	8
9. Verse	9
10. Verse	10
11. Verse	11
12. Verse	12
13. Verse	13
14. Verse	14
15. Verse	15
Verse	17
Verse	19
Verse	21

Preface

One summer day the rising sun announced the power of its glory to the east and as usual shone on the face of the earth, being the vehicle of nine unique diamonds in the universe forgeds in the bowels of Helios able to obtain by its nature true, the absolute glory in any hostile circumstance that will be presented by they descend to earth; those nine diamonds rose taking the bodily form of nine girls whose fascination from their place of origin impact warmly and subtly with their polyphony, the heart in the inhabitants of earth; the first opinions coincided in accepting their true identity as girls from the stars and honoring them as such; without waiting for, fake opinions dominated by uncontrolled anger that was supply with thoughts for having what belongs to others, and the non-acceptance of self-control in their hearts, they objected to the fascination of the stars that realized their dream of being part of humanity.

18 VERSES
THE
UNIVERSAL
STORY

THE NINE GIRLS FROM THE STARS
DOMINATE THE FEELINGS KEEPER

JOHN J. A. MARTZHALL

Copyright © John J. A. Martzhall
All Rights Reserved.

This book has been published with all efforts taken to make the material error-free after the consent of the author. However, the author and the publisher do not assume and hereby disclaim any liability to any party for any loss, damage, or disruption caused by errors or omissions, whether such errors or omissions result from negligence, accident, or any other cause.

While every effort has been made to avoid any mistake or omission, this publication is being sold on the condition and understanding that neither the author nor the publishers or printers would be liable in any manner to any person by reason of any mistake or omission in this publication or for any action taken or omitted to be taken or advice rendered or accepted on the basis of this work. For any defect in printing or binding the publishers will be liable only to replace the defective copy by another copy of this work then available.

Prologue

Nine pendants, masterpiece of the universal fountain, where gravitates the existence that respectfully observes beauty nine times exalted by its nature as girls from the stars, with the passing of time they understood the world around them while they remembered, that we are a reflection of many feelings; the feel is keeped with the thoughts that bloom in our minds like a pansy flower whose petals are "the feelings keepers" that descend to our hearts, reflecting fascinating colors being feelings materialized through a spontaneous reaction under unexpected circumstances; cunning with the silence of thoughts will persuade "the feelings keeper" in us.

1. VERSE

(Pansy green)

The universal utopia built by the consonance of nine joint degrees comprise the correct way to find the "feelings keeper" in the heart due to these constant changes or unexpected circumstances; nine beautiful girls of the stars with a magnificent electromagnetic power recognize the reaction in the beat of their hearts and persuade with benebolence to "the feelings keeper", who in an abstract context would exclaim to each girl of the stars:
I'm a reflection of yourself, I contemplate it in your eyes;
you achieve to be myself in unexpected circumstances,
it is cunning to silence the ideas of the mind while you breathe.
John J A Martzhall
69

2. VERSE

(Feel green)

Seven kingdoms coincided with each other; the nine girls from the stars have the capacity to take their place in the new world; Ionian, Doric, Phrygian, Lydian, Mixolid, Aeolian and Locrian observe with respect to Helios through nine fascinating forces of energy with the knowledge that Helios gave them, in the immensity; in unexpected circumstances "the feelings keeper" manifested in their hearts and yet each girl from the stars was prepared to differentiate herself from "the feelings keeper" while each of them thought:

I dispersed thoughts dominating the imagination
with the silence of thoughts, I understand the reaction
as something misleading quickly descending to my heart.
John J A Martzhall
69

3. VERSE

(Pansy red)

*Chamber of the Mixolydian Kingdom of the majestic Apollon;
harmony that in a ternary compass is used as the cradle of vocal
beauty, there the nine key signature are forged by the Volcanus
fire coming from the bowels of Helios, as investiture for the nine
girls from the stars; the subtle caress of the universal majesty is
her unconditional company, while in front of the brightness of her
eyes, "the feelings keeper" persuaded by the benevolence of the nine
girls from the stars, refutes in the abstract field of their minds:*
I'm a reflection of someone, you behave like other people,
they infuse thoughts in your mind, transformed by your
imagination;
you keep feelings in your heart, when you generates that
reaction.
John J A Martzhall
69

4. VERSE

(Feel red)

The humanity treasures the stars that contain Zeu's electromagnetic gift...

Glorious stars who upon arrival in strong time are manifest whit splendid wind instruments capable of traversing the galaxy in a blink, solving the tension generated by "the feelings keeper" that uncontrollably dominates each person inside by blossoming as a pansy flower in the vast field of their minds; the petals descend into their hearts as a reaction that generates spontaneous behaviors; the girls from the stars coincide while their radiant eyes are directed towards the sky next to the absolute power of the seven kingdoms contained in the diatonic scale that emanates from their nine voices:

my mind has moderate the thoughts with "the silence of thoughts,"
I dominate it is petals, being a flow'r of thoughts;
the reaction has bloomed in my mind to keep the feelings
John J A Martzhall
69

5. VERSE

(pansy orange)

Nine fascinating hearts that contain the warm virtue of dominance; three tones that on three occasions made a leap between the immensity of the universe and the strong time of the earth; nine girls from the stars who dominate within themselves "the feelings keeper"; extraordinary sources of electromagnetic power that are directed at the people:

I am a reflection all the time, it is "the feelings keeper,"
within your mind without autonomy, extending like water;
their colors reflect moods that cannot be dominated in you.
John J A Martzhall
69

6. VERSE

(Feel orange)

Moonlight... the arrival of a night diligently assured by Volcanus whose forge beautifies the mountains of unison that hold the imminent glory of the Phrygian kingdom; pansy flower that blooms in the abstract field of minds in nine precious treasures that the vulcan fire jealously protects; the nine girls from the stars raise their nine voices to the majesty of Helios:

I have contemplated in my heart to "the feelings keeper"
day and night, being the petals of the pansy flower;
while I breathe, my will dominates with the silence of thoughts.
John J A Martzhall
69

7. VERSE

(Pansy white)

How marvelous is the vastness of the universe, turning his attention to the earth he decided to decorate it with such precious treasures for humanity; Major and minor keys to twenty-four galaxies were given to the girls of the stars who took root on earth, when crossed the harmonic minor scale in a specific time signature, her eyes are able to decipher "the feelings keeper" that inhabits people; with a slight movement of factor fifth her delicate lips, container of an unimaginable power, instantly displace the unconditional company of the universal majesty to people who instruct:

I'm a reflection of yourself, I contemplate it in your heart,
you breathe willing to reflect a new reality to impart,
you perceive a white color in the petals of pansy flower
John J A Martzhall
69

8. VERSE

(Feel white)

Moonlight, sun in the night that bathes the perpendicular architecture of the earth, contemplated by the radiance of its beauty, home to the nine girls from the stars whose arduous task is to instruct people to dominate "the feelings keeper", by counteracting, an opaque space rock that at a distance from a half step earth, drives "the feelings keeper"out of control; nine precious harmonic voices with counterpoint admiration declaim to the immortal majesty of the universe:

From the sky, the brightness in the "black moon" is reflected
by the sweet taste of the only pleasant thought in my mind;
right now, throbbing white petals silence ideas like the wind.
John J A Martzhall
69

9. VERSE

(Pansy black)

Aurora borealis of meridion you are the solar wind of a powerful vocal instrument skillfully incorporated into the nine daughters of "Juventus" on earth; fascinating electromagnetic dome surrounds the nine girls from the stars , who move at the speed of light to share their art with the world:

I'm a reflection of someone, people's ideas persuade you…

people's moods and instincts come from their mem'ries, persuading you,

people's hearts, through "the feelings keeper" perceive the reality.

John J A Martzhall

69

10. VERSE

(Feel black)

Brave and unwavering "wisdom" she was forged by the immortal fire in the absolute majesty of the universe that watched with affection her birth; faithful friend of nine girls from the stars whose endowments is the stellar gift of a magnificent architect, with the purpose of dominating "the feelings keeper" who surrenders obediently to knowledge transmitted by the nine girls from the stars:

I have seen all colors of the pansy flower are moods,

my choice absorbs the ideas that pigment the "black moon"

the mood is reflected, through throbbing petals in my heart.

John J A Martzhall

69

11. VERSE

(Pansy yellow)

*A dim zodiacal light stands out on the night of the new moon,
favoring the hard work on earth of the nine girls from the stars,
while they contemplate the singularity of the twelve houses, cradle
of humanity where "the feelings keeper" resides, listening to her
nine dominant voices:
I'm a reflection all the time, your mind is a pansy "black moon"
it's black petals reflect moods, from your mind without autonomy,
whose iris of fire absorbs the ideas of reality
John J A Martzhall
69*

12. VERSE

Imperious austral summer that guarantees abundance, the universal promise of a glorious wind instrument with electromagnetic power; a work of art made as a pendant, which harmoniously amplifies the voice in the nine girls from the stars, whose repercussion, induces humanity by its nature to persuade "the feelings keeper" in their hearts; with giant steps the nine girls from the stars advance exclaiming...:

day and night throbbing in my heart, I see a dream come true;
like an instinctive sunrise of joy in summer, I move;
my autonomy pigments the black petals of yellow
John J A Martzhall
69

13. VERSE

(Pansy cian blue)

Selective pansies blossom in the minds of nine "girls from the stars", who share this talent in the first greenery of the north that precedes the arrival of a new reality, transported in high speed, through of a descending major scale, in response to the dominant cunning of a humanity that reflects its thoughts transformed into feelings; with satisfaction, the beauty of nine voices is heard:

I'm a reflection of yourself, you understand it cunningly,

all moods are transformed by thoughts infused into you, inevitably;

you perceive to "the feelings keeper" with your senses, through people.

John J A Martzhall

69

14. VERSE

(Feel cian blue)

Spring stands out in the soft and benevolent hands of the nine girls from the stars, while "the feelings keeper" persuaded by the dominance, bows; wearing its crimson petals emanating from its golden fire iris, being a pansy flower reflecting the infinite value of reciprocated love, revealed by the girls of the stars to humanity…:

its someone nice that I decided to frequent again,

I have contemplated scarlet petals throbbing in my heart,

while I dominate to "the feelings keeper" with my art.

John J A Martzhall

69

15. VERSE

(Pansy violet)

splendid girls from the stars, the experience of their humanity inspires the utopia promised to people, with the harmony of their nine voices that coincide:

I'm a reflection of someone who persuades... ¡the feelings keeper!; you used the senses, the silence of thoughts and your autonomy reflecting an original mood in your personality.

Time is rigorous when passing at great speed, any interval major or minor is impregnated with the experience of many events that make up the basis of eternity.

John J A Martzhall

69

Verse

(Feel violet)

Spectral violets illuminate the vast field of the mind, an autumnal experience acquired by the pendant forged in the sovereign fire of the universal empire; possession of the girls of the stars, who walk hand in hand with a united planet at the moment of listening to their nine voices sharing their harmonic balance...:

colors are transformed, being moods and instincts in people,
violet petals throb in my heart, it's a shared pansy
as they reflect the balance in their new reality.
John J A Martzhall
69

Verse

(Pansy dark blue)

The synchronism of the universal majesty is correct; nine galaxies dance in honor of the harmonic art that links a stellar coexistence between humanity and "the feelings keeper"; the nine girls from the stars have the respect of the eyes of the world along with the admiration of "the feelings keeper", promise of the winged fire incorporated in humanity, being words without sound rumbling inside:

I'm a reflection all the time, ¡the cunning in you fascinates!

day and night while you listen to melodies with precious voices;

I admire your conscience, you persuade me to reflect moods.

John J A Martzhall

69

Verse

(Feel dark blue)

In the remotest part of the vast winter field that constitutes the human mind, "the feelings keeper" will flourish impatiently like a pansy flower, reflecting from a fiery iris, dark blue petals pigmented by the domain exercised with the knowledge delivered to the world by the nine girls from the stars; From north to south, from east to west hundreds of thousands speak:

Again I would like to hear the sound of precious pansies,
being transformed feelings, through our voices with melodies
like a dream of blue petals throbbing in people's hearts.
John J A Martzhall
69